FAIRY PARTIES

Recipes, Crafts, and Games
for Enchanting Celebrations

BY
Colleen Mullaney

PHOTOGRAPHS BY
Jack Deutsch

CHRONICLE BOOKS
SAN FRANCISCO

This book is dedicated to my own little girls,
Grace and Katie, who have taught me you're never
too old to put on fairy wings and fly.
For, you never know where you might go.

Text copyright © 2010 by **COLLEEN MULLANEY**
Photographs copyright © 2010 by **JACK DEUTSCH**

Library of Congress Cataloging-in-Publication Data:
Mullaney, Colleen, 1966–
    Fairy parties : recipes, crafts, and games for enchanting celebrations / by Colleen Mullaney.
    —1st ed.
      p. cm.
    ISBN: 978-0-8118-6731-3
    1. Handicraft. 2. Children's parties. 3. Cookery. 4. Fairies in art. I. Title.

TT157.M776 2010
793.2'1—dc22

2009021469

Manufactured in China

Designed by **ALISON OLIVER**

10 9 8 7 6 5 4 3 2 1

Chronicle Books
680 Second Street
San Francisco, California 94107
www.chroniclebooks.com

table of
CONTENTS

OH, TO BE A FAIRY!

To wear beautiful wings and all magical things,
a shiny dress, oh yes, oh yes!
To have flowers in your crown as you dance all around,
and glittering shoes,
and be magic from your head to your toes.

A magic wand we will make,
but what fairy name will you take?
There are fairies for the earth, stars, flowers, and woods,
so choose what you like, all fairies are good!

And to play fairy games, and to dance in a ring—
oh, it's such fun to do fairy things.
So, let's not wait till it's late,
because of course there's fairy cake!
Sprinkled with rainbow pixie dust,
it truly is a fairy must!

Whatever you wish your fairy to be—
come, let's make that fairy be!

WHAT LITTLE GIRL DOESN'T DREAM of being a fairy? Fairies are the most enchanting of creatures—pretty, magical, and ever so clever. Fairies have been around for centuries, and they've never been more popular than they are today. Little girls love dressing up, parties, and sweet treats, so why not throw a fairy party and incorporate all three? With our lives going at one hundred miles an hour in a dozen different directions, planning a fairy party at home is the perfect way to spend time with your child and celebrate a birthday or holiday, or just have fun.

The parties in this book range from simple soirees for the younger set to parties for the more mature fairy. All of these fetes are aimed at girls from ages four to ten and include tasty treats everyone will love. The games and activities are simple enough to keep all the fairies focused and busy, whether they are sticking glitter letters onto a top, or pinning ribbon tails on a fairy wing. It's all imaginative fairy fun. Each of the five themed parties includes tips on decorating, fairy crafts and costumes, fairy activities, and fairy treats. But don't feel limited by these themes. You can mix and match any of the elements from the parties for your own personalized celebration. In addition, the "Fairy Crafts & Setting the Scene" and "Fairy Games" sections include more decorations and activities that you can add to your party to create a unique event.

Step-by-step directions make it easy to create charming fairy costumes for little sprites before the party; because what fairy is complete without a set of sparkly wings and a glittery wand? All sorts of fairy refreshments—both savory and sweet—are included in these pages to keep the fairies fueled for the festivities. And to help you set the scene, you'll learn how to fashion enchanted fairylands from wire hearts strung by satiny ribbons, paper stars, and the pièce de résistance: a tulle-covered bower in soft shades of pink.

FAIRY PARTY BASICS

TO START, DECIDE ON THE NUMBER of fairies you'll be hosting. Six girls is usually a good number, especially if all of the crafting and cooking is done by only one adult. (Some tips on time-savers and shortcuts follow.) The recipes and crafts throughout this book have directions and amounts for six fairies, but they can be increased or reduced as necessary.

Next, decide on a theme. The Fairy Sweet party is good for ages two to six; the Sugarplum Fairies party for ages four to eight; and the Rainbow Flower Fairies, Fairies Rock, and Woodland Fairies parties for ages six to ten. Or, look through the chapters and pick and choose crafts and activities you think will best suit your fairy guests. When setting a time for the party, keep in mind the age of the fairies. For the younger set, a lunch party—after the morning nap and before the afternoon cranky time—is ideal. Keep parties for the little ones on the shorter side, from an hour to an hour and a half. Late-afternoon or early-evening parties of up to two hours are suitable for older fairies. As long as they have costumes, treats, and games, they'll be happy!

Of course, you'll want to send invitations that give a sense of the wonders the party will hold. Look for colorful cards in stationery stores, or find sweet designs online that can be printed out in multiples. Choose a pretty font and colored ink to set a magical tone. In the invitation, be sure to suggest fairy-appropriate attire to match the theme. You might also want to give a brief outline of the activities and treats to be offered so that moms and guests will have an idea of what to expect. Before sealing the envelope, add a little paper confetti to each for a sprinkling of fairy dust. (A word to the wise: Avoid glitter, as it scatters everywhere and is nearly impossible to vacuum.)

After you've chosen the crafts, activities, and treats for your party, compile a comprehensive shopping list. Check the Resources section in the back of this book for helpful Web sites and a list of stores for fairy supplies.

The aim of this book is to inspire you, not to over-burden you with recipes to follow and decorations to make. Don't feel that you have to make everything for the party from scratch. Store-bought foods such as cakes and pastry shells are more than acceptable. The same goes for the fairy costumes: If you don't have time to stitch up six tulle skirts, pick them up at a party store. If you choose to make the projects, channel your creative side and have fun. The photos in the book are there to inspire and guide, but interpret them as you wish and make your own magic!

All of the costumes and many of the recipes in this book can be made ahead of time; so, to help things go smoothly, do as much of your preparation in advance as possible. Then you can focus on setting the scene for the festivities on the day of the party. Remember: The basic ingredients for all successful parties are the same no matter what—friends, fun, and good things to eat. If you make sure all three of those elements are in place, you're sure to have a magical event.

THE HISTORY OF FAIRIES

A FAIRY (also known as a *fay*, a *faerie*, or a *faery*) is a mythical creature with magical powers. Though we think of fairies as small winged sprites, in the past they sometimes took the form of tall, angel-like creatures or trolls, and they flew by magic arts, rather than with the wings they are portrayed as having today.

Many tales have been told of fairies, which have been icons throughout history. They appear as characters in stories from medieval times to today; they were particularly popular during the Victorian era.

Though human in appearance, fairies have supernatural abilities. They can fly, cast spells, and influence or fore-see the future.

But how did fairies come to be? According to J. M. Barrie, the author of *Peter Pan*, fairies appeared "when the first baby laughed for the first time, its laugh broke into a thousand pieces, and they all went skipping about . . ." But many cultures have stories of a race of magical "little people." The mythical Tuatha Dé Danann, or "people of Danu," who preceded the ancestors of today's Irish, were originally pagan gods and goddesses who were said to have come to Ireland from northern islands or the sky. After being defeated in battle, they retreated to live in the *sidhe*, the small hills and earthen burial mounds found all over the country. After this, they took on the name of their homes and became the *sidhe*, or fairy folk, who wore green clothing and lived underground.

In some folk tales, fairies were ghosts that had taken on the souls of the dead, and could only be seen by those gifted with the ability of "second sight." Others believed that fairies were a class of fallen angels, or even devils, for some fairies were thought to be the source of mischief and trickery, especially after the growth of Puritanism. They were blamed for tangling children's hair during the night, stealing small items, and leading travelers astray. Among the many famous works of literature featuring fairies is William Shakespeare's *A Midsummer Night's Dream*, which is set in a woodland and in fairyland on the night of the full moon. The cast of characters includes mortal beings and Oberon, the king of the fairies, and Titania, his queen.

No one knows how long fairy tales have existed, but stories of supernatural beings are as old as time. Today, a "fairy tale" means a story about any such creature, including trolls and giants, but the literary genre of fairy tales, based on oral folk stories, found fame in late-seventeenth-century France with La Fontaine and Charles Perrault, with the Brothers Grimm in Germany beginning in 1812, and later with Hans Christian Andersen, J. R. R. Tolkien, and of course, Walt Disney.

FAMOUS FAIRIES

WHO KNOWS HOW MANY FAIRIES flit around our world? Throughout history we've heard tales of so many that it's impossible to list them all. Here are the stories of some of the more famous ones:

TINKER BELL

Possibly the most famous fairy of all, Tinker Bell came to life in J. M. Barrie's stories of Peter Pan. She's Peter's good friend, ever jealous of Wendy. Her voice rings out like a tinkling bell and a sprinkle of her magic pixie dust can make you fly. With her magic wand, Tink, as she is affectionately known, led Peter Pan through Never Never Land and helped return Wendy and her brothers home safely. In her Disney incarnation, she wears a glittering green dress, ornate slippers, and a bow in her hair, and she is as mischievous as she is beautiful. When you spot a bright sparkle or flash of light, that just might be Tinker Bell flitting by.

THE FAIRY GODMOTHER

In fairy tales, the fairy godmother is a mentor who also has magical powers. She often helps a prince or princess make dreams come true by using her power to grant wishes. The best known of all is Cinderella's fairy godmother, who grants Cinderella a beautiful dress, a magical carriage, and glass slippers so she can attend the ball and meet her prince.

THE TOOTH FAIRY

This gentle fairy helps children give up their lost baby teeth. If a child puts the tooth under his or her pillow before going to sleep, the Tooth Fairy will take the tooth and leave a coin in its place.

THE SUGARPLUM FAIRY

In Peter Tchaikovsky's famous ballet *The Nutcracker*, the Sugarplum Fairy and her attendants welcome Clara at their court in the Land of Sweets. Beautiful costumes from Spain, Arabia, and China are worn by dancers representing coffee, tea, chocolate, and sugar candy. The Sugarplum Fairy and a group of ballerinas dressed as flowers dance the Waltz of the Flowers for Clara.

THE COTTINGLEY FAIRIES

These fairies were made famous thanks to five photographs taken in England in 1917 and 1920 by two young cousins, Elsie Wright and Frances Griffiths. The images depict the girls playing with two fairies. The photos sparked a decades-long debate about their authenticity, and earned the cousins widespread notoriety. Although the two admitted later that the photos were staged, they both insisted that they believed in fairies. The 1997 film, *Fairy Tale: A True Story*, was based on the Cottingley fairies.

Fairy SWEET

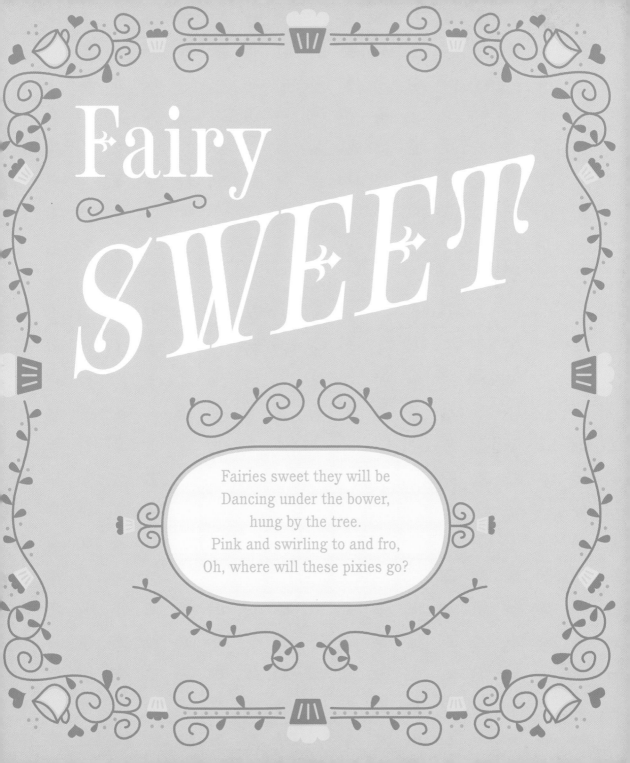

Fairies sweet they will be
Dancing under the bower,
hung by the tree.
Pink and swirling to and fro,
Oh, where will these pixies go?

AT THIS FAIRY PARTY,

sparkly pink fairies will dance about in a pastel dreamlike setting. Perfect for the younger set, this party features easy crafts, games, and a shorter timeline. It's ideal for fairies ages five and under, and is best in the afternoon hours, after naps and before dinner when the little sprites are happy and energetic.

Once the little ones have arrived and have changed into their fairy-sweet costumes, they can begin crafting hair clips for perfect crowning accents to wear in their hair and to have as a lovely party keepsake to take home.

Next, the pixies will parade into a fairy bower, where they'll find treats to savor. After feasting on tea sandwiches, cupcakes, and pixie punch, it's time for fairy games.

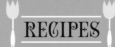

COSTUMES

Blooming Barrettes
Blossom Tops
Blossom Slippers
Tutus
Fairy Wings

CRAFTS/GAMES

Wands
Fairy Godmother Says
Fairy Freeze Dance

RECIPES

Pixie Punch
Heart-Shaped Tea Sandwiches
Cupcakes in Bloom
Meringue Blossoms

YOU'LL CREATE AN ENCHANTED FAIRY BOWER, which, as fairy lore states, is a magical retreat for tiny sprites. This bower holds a table filled with treats and sweets, all in shades of pink. The hideaway is covered in layers of pink tulle, draped like the sugared icing on cupcakes. Puffs of pink tulle blossoms adorn the outside, and ribbons and tulle blossoms are the perfect finishing touches. The bower is hung from a tree, patio arbor, or trellis, so that it has plenty of room for the tulle sides to hang freely (for complete instructions on how to make the bower, see page 129).

BLOOMING BARRETTES

The fairies will have a ball crafting these flower-laden hair clips. They'll simply glue lengths of pink ribbon to the frame, then top the clip with tiny faux blossoms. These make whimsical party gifts and fun souvenirs of the day.

· ·

MAKES 6 BARRETTES

You will need

Scissors

2 yd/180 cm 3/8-in-/1-cm-wide light pink grosgrain ribbon

6 plain metal barrettes

2 yd/180 cm 3/8-in-/1-cm-wide medium pink grosgrain ribbon

Aleene's Tacky Glue

2 stems fabric cherry blossoms

1. With the scissors, cut a piece of the light pink ribbon to fit the length of the barrette. Glue it to the top and let dry. After all of the barrettes have been covered with ribbon, cut the remaining light pink ribbon and the medium pink ribbon into 6-in/15-cm lengths and glue 5 strands onto the center of each barrette for streamers.

2. Glue the flowers onto the barrette in a pleasing pattern. Let dry. Glue a blossom or two onto random streamers to finish.

BLOSSOM TOPS

Give simple pink tops a collar of blooms and
loops of ribbons for a look that's sure to delight.

MAKES 6 TOPS

You will need

6 light pink knit tops

36 pink fabric hydrangea blossoms

Hot-glue gun

Glue sticks

3 yd/270 cm ½-in-/12-mm-wide
   light green wire-edged ribbon

1. Place a top on your work surface.

2. Arrange 6 blossoms around the front collar of the top.
   Glue in place. Let dry.

3. Cut the ribbon into six 18-in/45-cm lengths. Make small
   loops with the ribbon, working it around the blossoms.
   Hot-glue in place. Let dry.

BLOSSOM SLIPPERS

Festoon soft pink ballerina slippers with small bunches
of faux flowers. These slippers give fairies special powers
to dance and sing in the fairy ring.

MAKES 6 PAIRS OF SLIPPERS

You will need

Scissors

6 small, wire-stemmed
decorative flowers (found
in bridal sections of
craft stores)

6 pairs pink ballerina slippers

Hot-glue gun

Glue sticks

1. Using the scissors, cut the wires from the flowers.

2. Place a flower on the top center of a slipper. Hot-glue
in place. Let dry.

3. Repeat with the remaining slippers and flowers.

COSTUME

TUTUS

These delightful little skirts will thrill any fairy. They are
easily made by sewing together layers of tulle and shimmery fabric,
then embellishing them with faux blossoms and ribbons.

MAKES 6 SKIRTS

You will need

Scissors

3 yd/270 cm 36-in-/90-cm-wide
light pink pearlized sheer fabric

3 yd/270 cm 36-in-/90-cm-wide
pink tulle (found in rolls in
craft stores)

3 yd/270 cm 36-in-/90-cm-wide
pink satin lining fabric

Straight pins

Sewing machine

4 yd/360 cm ¾-in-/
2-cm-wide elastic

Safety pin

Sewing needle

Light pink thread

Fabric blossoms

1. With the scissors, cut all the fabrics into pieces that are
18 in/46 cm long. On a work surface, layer them, with the
pearlized fabric on the bottom, then a layer of tulle, then
the satin lining on top. Fold the top over to make a 1-in/
2.5-cm top hem that will become the waistband and pin
through all three layers. Using the sewing machine, stitch
along the pins to make a top hem.

2. Cut the elastic into six 24-in/60-cm lengths. Using the safety
pin fastened to one end of the elastic, slide the elastic through
the top hem that will become the waist band. To sew side
seams, fold the skirt in half lengthwise and pin the sides
together, leaving a 1-in/2.5-cm seam. Stitch along the pins.
Remove the pins and turn the skirt right-side out.

3. Every 6 or 8 in/15 or 20 cm, along the bottom hem, gather
the fabrics up by 4 in/10 cm and stitch them together with the
needle and thread. Stitch a fabric blossom on top of each puff.

TIME-SAVER: If you don't have time to sew, you can find
plain pink tutus or ballerina skirts at large retailers. Then
simply gather the fabric, stitch to make the puffs, and adorn
the puffs with blossoms.

FAIRY WINGS

Embellishing store-bought wings with faux flowers and a
bow of tulle turns the ordinary into the extraordinary in a short
amount of time and with very little effort and expense.

MAKES 6 PAIRS OF WINGS

You will need

6 stems pink fabric
   delphinium blossoms

Hot-glue gun

Glue sticks

6 pairs pink netted
   store-bought wings

Scissors

7 yd/630 cm 6-in-/15-cm-wide
   white tulle (found in rolls
   in craft stores)

1. Remove the blossoms from the stems. Hot-glue the blossoms
   onto a pair of wings in a pleasing pattern.

2. Using the scissors, cut the tulle into seven 1-yd/90-cm
   lengths. Fold six pieces, accordion-style, into 6-in/
   15-cm bundles. Cut the remaining strip into 6-in/15-cm
   lengths, and tie one around the center of each bundle.

3. Fluff and arrange each bundle to create large puffs.

4. Glue a tulle puff to the center of where a pair of wings join
   and let dry. Adorn the tulle with blossoms as well.

5. Repeat with the remaining puffs, blossoms, and pairs
   of wings.

CRAFT

WANDS

Charming wands, made from simple Styrofoam balls covered
with delicate faux flowers, wrapped with ribbons, and tied with a tulle bow,
are perfect for casting spells and granting wishes.

MAKES 6 WANDS

You will need

White spray paint

Three 30-in/76-cm ³/₈-in-/1-cm-wide
wooden dowels

Sharp scissors

Six 2-in-/5-cm-diameter
Styrofoam balls

3 stems pink fabric
cherry blossoms

Aleene's Tacky Glue

2 yd/180 cm 6-in-/15-cm-wide white
tulle (found in rolls at craft stores)

2 yd/180 cm ½-in-/12-mm-wide
pink-and-white gingham ribbon

1. Spray paint the dowels white. Let dry. Using the scissors, cut
each dowel into two 15-in/38-cm lengths. Anchor a Styrofoam
ball onto each dowel by pushing the ball firmly down so that
the dowel goes into the ball about 2 in/5 cm.

2. Remove the fabric blossoms from the stems. Apply glue
generously to a small area on the ball and press down a
blossom firmly to affix it. Continue until the ball is completely
covered in blossoms. Repeat with the remaining balls and
blossoms. Let dry.

3. Cut the tulle and ribbon into six 12-in/30-cm lengths.
Tie a tulle length and ribbon length around each wand under
the ball.

FAIRY GODMOTHER SAYS

1. This is the fairy version of Simon Says. The adult, wearing a crown or holding a wand, directs the children to do as the fairy godmother says. For example, "Fairy Godmother says to touch your wand to your head, then dance around."

2. The fairies that dance around without touching their wands to their heads first are eliminated because they didn't do what the Fairy Godmother told them to do.

3. The last fairy remaining is the winner. This game is both fun and short, making it perfect for young fairies.

FAIRY FREEZE DANCE

1. Choose some fun fairy music (see page 142). When the music plays, the fairies dance.

2. When it stops, they freeze and must remain perfectly still until the music starts again. Any fairy who doesn't remain still is eliminated.

3. The last remaining fairy is the winner.

PIXIE PUNCH

This colorful, sparkling punch will be
a sure hit at a fairy party. It's so easy to make
that you can do it at the very last minute.

. . . .

SERVES 6 FAIRIES

Ingredients

Lemon wedge

Pink sugar sprinkles

1 liter strawberry- or
    lemon-flavored sparkling
    water, chilled

1 liter pink lemonade, chilled

4 cups/500 g ice cubes

6 fresh strawberries, hulled
    and quartered (optional)

1. Wet the rims of six glasses by rubbing them with
   the lemon wedge. Pour the sugar sprinkles into a
   saucer and dip the moistened rim of each glass into
   the sugar to coat.

2. In a punch bowl, combine the sparkling water and
   lemonade. Add the ice cubes.

3. To serve, ladle the punch into each prepared glass and
   drop in four strawberry quarters, if you like.

HEART-SHAPED TEA SANDWICHES

A heart-shaped cookie cutter transforms simple sandwiches into special fairy treats. Make these sandwiches just before the party to ensure freshness.

MAKES 12 OPEN-FACE SANDWICHES; SERVES 6 FAIRIES

Ingredients

12 thin sandwich slices mild cheese, such as Monterey Jack

12 slices whole-grain bread

Unsalted butter, at room temperature

12 thin slices cucumber

6 cherry tomatoes, stemmed and halved

1. Place a slice of cheese on top of a slice of bread and, using the heart-shaped cookie cutter, press down until the bread and cheese are cut out. Continue with the remaining bread and cheese slices.

2. Remove a cheese slice from a piece of bread and spread butter on the bread, add the cheese on top, add a slice of cucumber, and top with a cherry tomato half.

3. Repeat with the remaining sandwiches. Place on a platter and serve immediately.

CUPCAKES IN BLOOM

What's a party without cake? Delicate garden
blossoms top these little ones. Look in your produce section
(or your garden) for pesticide-free edible blossoms.

MAKES 18 CUPCAKES

Ingredients

2 ¾ cups/345 g all-purpose plain flour

1 tsp baking powder

½ tsp baking soda/bicarbonate
of soda

1 tsp salt

1 cup/225 g unsalted butter,
at room temperature

2 cups/400 g granulated sugar

4 large eggs, at room temperature

1 tsp vanilla extract/essence

¾ cup/180 ml buttermilk

1. Preheat the oven to 350°F/180°C. Line 18 standard muffin
cups with paper liners.

2. In a large bowl, combine the flour, baking powder, baking
soda/bicarbonate of soda, and salt. Stir with a whisk
to blend.

3. In another large bowl, cream the butter and granulated
sugar until light and fluffy. Beat in the eggs one at a time.
Beat in the vanilla. Beat in the dry ingredients alternately
with the buttermilk in two increments until blended,
scraping down the sides and bottom of the bowl once
or twice.

4. Fill each lined muffin cup three-fourths full. Bake for 18 to
25 minutes, or until golden brown and a toothpick inserted
in the center of a cupcake comes out clean. Let cool in the
pan for 10 minutes, then transfer the cupcakes from the pan
to a wire rack and let cool completely.

(continued)

Ingredients

VANILLA ICING

½ cup/115 g unsalted butter,
   at room temperature

1 ½ tsp vanilla extract/essence

3 cups/300 g confectioners'/icing
   sugar, sifted

3 Tbsp water

Drop of pink or green food
   coloring (optional)

18 edible flowers, such as violets,
   pansies, or violas

Water for brushing

Superfine/castor sugar for sprinkling

5. **FOR THE ICING:** In a medium bowl, combine the butter and vanilla and stir until smooth. Stir in the confectioners'/icing sugar 1/2 cup/65 g at a time alternating with the water until fluffy and smooth. Add the food coloring (if using) and stir to blend evenly. Using a frosting knife, palette knife, or dinner knife, frost the cupcakes.

6. Using a pastry brush, brush the edible flowers lightly with water. Sprinkle the flowers with superfine/castor sugar to coat lightly. Let dry.

7. Place a sugared flower in the center of each cupcake and serve.

RECIPE

MERINGUE BLOSSOMS

Wave your magic wand and cook up these melt-in-your-mouth perfections. Easy to make, they are a delightful party treat. They can be made several days ahead and stored in an airtight container for up to 4 days.

Note: To make these, you will need a plastic pastry bag and an open star decorating tip (found in cookware stores and the baking aisle of most craft stores).

SERVES 6 FAIRIES

Ingredients

3 large egg whites

¾ cup / 150 g sugar

¼ tsp cream of tartar

1 tsp vanilla extract/essence

Red food coloring

Water for brushing

Pink and green sugar sprinkles
for decorating

1. Preheat the oven to 250°F/120°C. Line two baking sheets with parchment paper.

2. In a large bowl, beat the egg whites with an electric mixer on medium speed until soft peaks form. Gradually beat in the sugar, 1 tablespoon at a time. Beat in the cream of tartar and vanilla. Continue beating until stiff, glossy peaks form. Using one very small drop at a time, fold in the red food coloring with a rubber spatula until the mixture is a pale pink.

3. Spoon the mixture (in batches if necessary) into a plastic pastry bag fitted with an open star tip and form large S shapes on the prepared baking sheets. Place in the oven and bake for 1 hour. Turn off the oven and leave the oven door closed for at least 10 minutes. Remove from the oven and let cool completely on the pan. Using a pastry brush, paint each meringue very lightly with water and sprinkle with sugar crystals.

Sugar-PLUM FAIRIES

Oh, to be a fairy
In the Land of Sweets
Dancing in a ballet skirt
And eating special treats.

CREATING A SUGARPLUM FAIRY PARTY

is a delight. What little girl wouldn't want to be dressed in shimmery shades of lavender, wearing fancy ballerina slippers and a sparkly headpiece?

This party begins with the transformation of little girls into fairies as they change into their beautiful outfits. Once dressed, the fairies begin crafting the wands that will bring them magical powers. This is a great arrival activity, and each fairy can take home her wand as a special keepsake. After the wands are finished and the fairy outfits are complete, the Sugarplums enter the Land of Sweets, where they'll find many special treats.

Once full, the fairies head out to their garden court to dance and play games, including Pass the Parcel and Musical Wands (the Sugarplum version of Musical Chairs). At last, the tired fairies dance off into the night with memories of a magical afternoon.

COSTUMES

Flower-Encrusted Crowns

Sparkly Skirts

Bejeweled Tops

Dancing Shoes

CRAFTS/GAMES

Whimsical Wands

Pass the Parcel

Musical Wands

RECIPES

Berry Smoothies

Pixie Rolls

Fruit Tartlets

setting the
SCENE

THE LAND OF SWEETS IS AN ENCHANTED PLACE for the fairies to frolic about in and enjoy their treats. String paper lanterns with ribbons from white lattice to evoke a ceiling that seems to dance on air. Here, the lattice is simply hung from an outdoor play set, but can easily be fastened to an awning or a canopy. Fashion lengths of tulle in the trees for a soft backdrop. Set the table with ribbons streaming across the top and cascading to the floor for a lavish effect. Bedeck the chairs with bows of tulle to give each fairy a special place to sit. Scatter faux blossoms in lavender hues on the ground for a sprinkling of magic.

FLOWER-ENCRUSTED CROWNS

Decorative jeweled garland lengths make the easy-to-twist bases
for the headpieces. Faux blossoms in purple tones are wired on, and ribbon
in shades of purple are tied on to finish the bejeweled crowns.

MAKES 6 CROWNS

You will need

Scissors

3 yd/270 cm jeweled garland
(found in craft stores)

2 stems lavender fabric
delphinium blossoms

2 periwinkle fabric
delphinium blossoms

Wire cutters

Silver florist's wire

4 yd/360 cm ¼-in-/6-mm-wide
lavender satin ribbon

4 yd/360 cm ¼-in-/6-mm-wide
purple satin ribbon

1. Using the scissors, cut the jeweled garland into six 18-in/
45-cm lengths. Twist the ends in a loop to secure.

2. Remove the fabric blossoms from their stems. Using the wire
cutters, cut the floral wire into 4-in/10-cm lengths. Wind a
wire around the base of each blossom. Wire the blossoms to
the garland by twisting the ends to secure.

3. Cut both the lavender ribbon and the purple ribbon into six
24-in/60-cm lengths. At the back of each crown, tie one
lavender and one purple ribbon on for streamers.

SPARKLY SKIRTS

The sparkles mimic the glistening sugar coating of sugarplums.
The skirts are made of petal shapes with layers of lining, tulle, and shimmering
fabric, to give the illusion of flower blossoms swaying in the breeze.

MAKES 6 SKIRTS

You will need

Craft paper

Pencil

Fabric marker

3 yd/270 cm 36-in-/90-cm-wide
    lavender satin fabric lining

Scissors

3 yd/270 cm 36-in-/90-cm-wide
    lavender tulle (found in rolls
    in craft stores)

3 yd/270 cm 36-in-/90-cm-wide
    lavender pearlized sheer fabric

3 yd/270 cm 36-in-/90-cm-wide
    lavender iridescent satin fabric

Straight pins

Sewing machine

Matching thread

4 yd/360 cm ¾-in-/
    2-cm-wide elastic

Safety pin

1. On a piece of craft paper, draw a rectangle that is 12 in/30 cm wide by 16 in/40 cm long. Using the pencil, mark the midpoints of each side. Starting at the midpoint of the top (12 in/30 cm side), draw a leaf shape coming out to the midpoint of the long side and then back to the midpoint of the short side. Cut out the leaf and use as template.

2. On a work surface, using the fabric marker, trace 30 petal shapes onto the fabric lining. Be sure to trace the shapes close together to ensure 30 petals. Using the scissors, cut out the petal shapes.

3. Repeat the above step with the three remaining fabrics.

4. Layer five cutout petal shapes of each kind of fabric on a work surface with the leaf tips pointed in one direction, with the fabric layered in this order: pearlized fabric, iridescent fabric, tulle, and satin lining.

5. Fold over the top edges of the fabrics by 1 in/2.5 cm. Pin in place. Using the sewing machine, sew along the pinned edge. Cut the elastic into six 24-in/60-cm lengths. Using the safety pin fastened to one end of the elastic, slide the elastic through the top hem. Sew the ends of the elastic together to finish, and fluff the petals.

COSTUME

BEJEWELED TOPS

These simple white tank tops are adorned with
pink, purple, and silver jewels in simple patterns fashioned
after ballerinas dancing through the air.

MAKES 6 TOPS

You will need

6 white tank tops

Large and small decorative pink,
purple, and silver gems
(found in craft stores)

E-6000 Glue

1. Place a tank top on a work surface.

2. Arrange the large gems around the shirt to become the
centers of the bursts (as shown in the photo). Glue in place.

3. Arrange the smaller gems in swirling patterns around the
larger gems. Let dry for about 5 minutes.

DANCING SHOES

These sparkling slippers, adorned with
faux blossoms, can be worn again and again for
holidays, parties, and fairy dress-up.

MAKES 6 PAIRS OF SLIPPERS

You will need

Scissors

2 packages mini hydrangea
    floral picks

Large decorative purple gems
    (found in craft stores)

6 pairs white ballet slippers
    to fit the fairies

Hot-glue gun

Glue sticks

1. Using the scissors, cut the stems off the floral picks.
   Arrange the flowers and gems on the top of a ballet
   slipper in a pleasing pattern.

2. Hot-glue in place. Repeat with the matching slipper.

3. Repeat with the remaining pairs of slippers.

WHIMSICAL WANDS

The fairies will glue the sparkling gems on both sides
of these purple star-shaped wands. Next, they will add ruffles made from
precut tulle circles. They will finish by tying on colorful ribbons, and presto!
In minutes, an ordinary store-bought wand becomes magical.

· · · · · · · · · · · · · · · · · · ⭐ · · · · · · · · · · · · · · · · · ·

MAKES 6 WANDS

You will need

Aleene's Tacky Glue

240 Decorative silver gems
(found in craft stores)

6 purple wands with star-shaped
foam tops (found in party
supply and craft stores)

Scissors

30 precut 9-in-/23-cm-diameter
lavender tulle rounds with
decorative ruffle edging
(found in craft stores)

3 yd/270 cm $3/8$-in-/1-cm-wide
lavender satin ribbon

3 yd/270 cm $3/8$-in-/1-cm-wide
purple satin ribbon

1. Glue about 20 decorative gems on one side of each foam
star. Let dry. Repeat on the other side of the star.

2. Using the scissors, cut a $1/4$-in/6-mm square in the center
of five tulle rounds. Push the bottom of a wand through
and bunch the rounds together at the top. Repeat with
the remaining wands and tulle.

3. Cut the lavender and purple ribbons into 12-in/30-cm
lengths. Wrap three purple and/or lavender ribbons around
the bunched tulle and tie a knot to secure the ribbons
and tulle to the wand.

PASS THE PARCEL

1. For this game, you'll need as many prizes as there are players: one for the winner, wrapped in as many layers of wrapping paper as there are players; and smaller prizes (such as candies, stickers, pencils, etc.) for each of the other players.

2. Wrap the main prize in bright festive paper, so all the children know which is the last round. Wrap the smaller prizes in subsequent layers of paper around the main prize, with the next small prize on top of the previous layer.

3. Sit the fairies in a circle and hand the wrapped parcel to a player. Start the fairy music (see page 142). The parcel is passed around the ring until the music stops. The fairy holding the parcel when the music stops unwraps a layer of paper, revealing a small prize.

4. When the music starts again, the passing resumes. Repeat until each player has had a turn at unwrapping a layer (an adult is needed to supervise this part!) and the last fairy unwraps the main prize.

MUSICAL WANDS

1. For this game, you'll need a wand for each player and more fairy music (see page 142). Arrange the wands in a circle on the ground and start the music.

2. The fairies dance around the wands until the music stops and they must find a wand to sit next to. At the beginning of each round, a wand is removed, and the fairy with no wand when the music stops is out.

3. The winner is the last fairy left with a wand.

BERRY SMOOTHIES

Even fairies need their vitamins, and these smoothies
are filled with goodness to give them energy for games and dancing.
Decorative straws topped with foam-cut flowers are
the perfect finishing touches for these colorful treats.

SERVES 6 FAIRIES

Ingredients

2 bananas, peeled and cut
   into slices

1 cup/125 g frozen blueberries

1 cup/125 g frozen raspberries

½ cup/60 g frozen strawberries

1 cup/240 ml sweetened
   cranberry juice

2 cups/250 g crushed ice

6 Flower straws

1. In a blender, combine all the ingredients and blend
   until smooth.

2. Pour the smoothies into cups and serve immediately
   with the straws.

NOTE: If the consistency is too thick, add a little more
cranberry juice. If too runny, add a little more ice.
Blend again.

FLOWER STRAWS

Using dark purple, medium purple, and light purple foam
sheets, cut 6 flower shapes from each so there are 18
flowers total. Punch a hole in the center of each shape and
layer one of each shade of purple to form 6 flowers. Insert
one end of a bendable white straw through the holes.

PIXIE ROLLS

These bite-size rolls, sprinkled with lavender-colored sugar,
are just right for busy fairies. They can be made in no time at all, even with
a house full of sugarplum fairies. There is a sprinkling of fun in every roll.

. . . . ✦ . . . .

MAKES 12 ROLLS; SERVES 6 FAIRIES

Ingredients

¼ cup/75 g raspberry jam

¼ cup/75 g blackberry jam

6 slices white bread,
     crusts removed

Lavender sugar sprinkles

1. In a small bowl, stir the jams together.

2. Spread the jam mixture evenly on one side of each bread
   slice and roll each slice on a flat surface.

3. Place on a cutting board, seam-side down, and cut each roll
   in half crosswise.

4. Place, seam-side down, on a decorative plate or platter.
   Sprinkle lightly with the colored sugar.

VARIATION: For added texture, mix ¼ cup/2 oz room-
temperature cream cheese into the jam mixture before
spreading on the bread.

RECIPE

FRUIT TARTLETS

Fairies love these pretty little tarts. The colorful
berries are nestled in a crust filled with vanilla pudding.

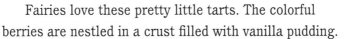

MAKES 12 TARTLETS; SERVES 6 FAIRIES

Ingredients

VANILLA PUDDING

2 cups/480 ml whole milk

¾ cup/150 g granulated sugar

6 large egg yolks

2 Tbsp all-purpose/plain flour

2 tsp vanilla extract/essence

1 package (12 oz/375 g)
  refrigerated pastry dough

1 cup/250 g fresh blueberries

1 cup/250 g fresh blackberries

1 cup/250 g fresh raspberries

1 cup/250 g seedless red grapes

1 cup/220 g superfine/castor
  sugar for coating

1. **FOR THE PUDDING:** In a medium saucepan, heat the milk over medium heat until bubbles form around the edges of the pan. Remove from the heat. In a medium bowl, whisk together the sugar and egg yolks until light in color. Whisk in the flour. Gradually whisk some of the hot milk into the egg yolk mixture. Return to the saucepan and cook over low heat, stirring constantly, for 5 minutes, or until thickened. Do not boil. Remove from the heat and stir in the vanilla. Pour into a bowl and press plastic wrap directly onto the surface. Let cool. Refrigerate at least 1 hour.

2. Preheat the oven to 350°F/180°C. Roll out the pastry dough on a floured surface. Using a flower-shaped cookie cutter, cut out twelve shapes. Press the flowers gently into twelve standard muffin cups and bake for 15 minutes, or until set and lightly golden. Check halfway through baking and, if the centers are puffy, press them down using a spoon. Remove from the oven and let cool completely in the pans on wire racks. Pop the crusts out of the muffin cups.

3. Sprinkle the fruit with water, then roll in the superfine/castor sugar to coat. Set aside. Fill the pastry cups with pudding and place the sugared fruit on top. Refrigerate until ready to serve, up to 24 hours.

Rainbow FLOWER FAIRIES

How to summon a flower fairy?
You could, I suppose,
Sit quietly among the garden flowers
Where the lily meets the rose.
Or you could pick some daisies
The color of the sun
And wish and wish upon them
For a flower fairy to come.

THIS ENCHANTING PARTY will bring a

bouquet of rainbow flower fairies to your garden. Each fairy is dressed as a different flower, in costumes inspired by a garden's rainbow hues: a pink rose, a blue lily, an orange zinnia, a green gerbera daisy, a purple pansy, and a yellow daisy.

For this outdoor party, greet the flower fairies in a garden decorated with magic stars in rainbow hues. Upon arrival, the hosting fairy bestows a color and name on each of her friends. The shirts become keepsakes that each flower fairy will take home.

COSTUMES

Blossoming Headbands
Petal Skirts
Glitter Tops
Garden Shoes

CRAFTS/GAMES

Rainbow Wands
Garden, Garden, Flower
Sardines

RECIPES

Lemon-Lime Sparkling Punch
Fruit Kabobs
Sweet Roll Flowers
Fairy Bread
Fairy Bars
Rainbow Parfaits

FOR THIS FAIRY GARDEN PARTY, hang paper stars made from colorful paper bags (see page 132) from tree branches, a patio awning, or an arbor. The table is filled with rainbow-inspired treats and wrapped with festive ribbons. Each flower fairy has her own set of accessories—a wand, a headband, and garden shoes—in the fairy's own special color.

BLOSSOMING HEADBANDS

These are the perfect finishing touch
for a head-to-toes flower ensemble.

. . . . ✿ . . . .

MAKES 6 HEADBANDS

You will need

6 fabric flowers: 1 pink rose,
   1 blue lily, 1 green gerbera,
   1 yellow daisy, 1 purple pansy,
   and 1 orange zinnia

Hot-glue gun

Glue sticks

½ yd/45 cm ½-in-/12-mm-wide
   grosgrain ribbon in *each* color:
   pink, blue, green, yellow, purple,
   and orange

6 white satin headbands (found in
   craft stores)

1. Remove the flowers from the stems.

2. Glue one end of a ribbon to the inside of a headband.
   Wrap the ribbon around the headband from one end to
   the other to cover the headband completely. Cut and glue
   the end of the ribbon to hold in place. Repeat with the
   remaining headbands and ribbons.

3. Glue a blossom to each headband in the ten o'clock position.
   Let dry.

PETAL SKIRTS

Made from crushed velvet with a tulle underlining in bright garden hues,
these skirts make twirling about even more fun.

MAKES 6 SKIRTS

You will need

Scissors

3 yd/270 cm 36-in-/270-cm-wide tulle in *each* color: pink, blue, orange, green, purple, yellow (found in rolls in craft stores)

3 yd/270 cm 36-in-/270-cm-wide crushed velvet in *each* color: pink, blue, orange, green, purple, yellow

Straight pins

Sewing machine

Matching thread

5 yd/450 cm ¾-in-/2-cm-wide elastic

Safety pin

1. Using the scissors, cut each piece of tulle and velvet into six 18-in-/45-cm-long pieces.

2. Lay a piece of velvet, pile-side down, on a work surface. Add the matching color of tulle on top. Fold under and pin a 1-in/2.5-cm hem at the top for the waistband. Using the sewing machine, stitch along the pins. Remove the pins. Repeat with the remaining tulle and velvet.

3. Cut the elastic into six 30-in/75-cm lengths. Using the safety pin fastened to one end of the elastic, slide a length of elastic through the hems of each petal of a specific color. Fold the fabrics over lengthwise and pin the sides and elastic together to make a 1-in/2.5-cm seam. Sew the side seam closed. Turn the skirt right-side out.

4. Repeat with the remaining colors.

GLITTER TOPS

Positive words spread a positive
message, especially glittery ones!

· ❀ ·

MAKES 6 TOPS

You will need

6 fitted white T-shirts

Adhesive glitter letters
(found in craft stores) to spell
Blossom, *Shine*, *Sparkle*,
Dazzle, *Believe*, and *Dream*.

1. Lay a T-shirt on a work surface. Place letters to spell
one of the words in the center of a top. Following the
manufacturer's instructions, affix the letters.

2. Repeat to decorate the remaining 5 tops.

GARDEN SHOES

These blossom-adorned shoes will keep your
fairies skipping through the flowers all day.

· · · · · · · · · · · · · · · · · ❀ · · · · · · · · · · · · · · · · ·

MAKES 6 PAIRS OF SHOES

You will need

2 *each* fabric blossoms: pink
roses, blue lilies, green
gerberas, yellow daisies, purple
pansies, and orange zinnias

Hot-glue gun

Glue sticks

6 pairs skips or white sneakers to
fit the fairies

1. Remove the flowers from the stems.

2. Glue one of the two matching flowers to the top of each
shoe in a pair. Let dry.

RAINBOW WANDS

These colorful wands can cast
any number of spells.

MAKES 6 WANDS

You will need

Sharp scissors

Three 30-in/76-cm ³⁄₈-in-/1-cm-thick
    wooden dowels

Silver florist's wire

12 fabric flowers: 2 pink rose,
    2 blue lily, 2 green gerbera,
    2 purple pansy, 2 yellow daisy,
    and 2 orange zinnia

Hot-glue gun

Glue sticks

6 yd/540 cm ½-in-/12-mm-wide
    green grosgrain ribbon

1 yd/90 cm ³⁄₈-in-/1-cm-wide
    ribbon in *each* color: pink,
    blue, green, purple, yellow,
    and orange

1. Using the scissors, cut each dowel into two 15-in/38-cm lengths. Using the florist's wire, wire two of the same color of blossom onto the top of each dowel.

2. Hot-glue a green grosgrain ribbon to the top of each dowel and wrap the ribbon around the dowel until it is covered. Cut off any excess ribbon and hot-glue to the bottom of the dowels.

3. Cut each ribbon in half and tie the matching color to each wand just under the blossom.

GARDEN, GARDEN, FLOWER

For the garden version of Duck, Duck, Goose, the fairies sit in a circle. The fairy who is "it" goes around the circle saying, "Garden, garden, flower," and the fairy she calls "flower" must get up and chase her around the ring before she returns safely to the starting spot. If the first fairy is caught by the chasing fairy, she is out of the game. The last fairy to remain is the winner. This game is perfect for working up an appetite!

SARDINES

1. A version of hide-and-seek where the girl who is "it" hides and everyone else looks for her.

2. When each girl finds "it," she hides with her, and soon those who are left are looking for a hiding spot with the rest of the girls.

3. The last one to find the group gets to be "it" and hides for the next game.

LEMON-LIME SPARKLING PUNCH

Blossoming with fresh citrus zing,
this pixie punch is a party pleaser!

SERVES 6 FAIRIES

Ingredients

one can frozen lemonade
    concentrate, thawed

one can frozen limeade
    concentrate, thawed

two 1-liter bottles lemon flavored
    seltzer, chilled

4 cups ice

  Lemon and lime slices
    for garnish

Pour the thawed concentrates in a punch bowl, add the seltzer and mix well. Add the ice cubes, garnish with lemon and lime slices, and serve.

RECIPE

FRUIT KABOBS

Fresh fruit kabobs keep fairies healthy
and happy, with lots of energy to dance and play.

· · · · · · · · · · · · · · · · · · · ❀ · · · · · · · · · · · · · · · · · · ·

MAKES 24 KABOBS

Ingredients

1 cantaloupe/rock melon,
    peeled and seeded

1 honeydew melon, peeled
    and seeded

1 pineapple, peeled and cored

3 kiwifruits, peeled and sliced

1 bunch red seedless grapes,
    stemmed

2 cups/250 g fresh strawberries,
    hulled

1. Cut the melons and pineapple into 1-in/2.5-cm chunks.

2. Thread each kind of fruit alternately on each of two dozen long wooden skewers.

3. Serve immediately, or cover and refrigerate for up to 24 hours.

RECIPE

SWEET ROLL FLOWERS

Flower-shaped cinnamon buns made with bananas, raisins,
and dried apricots have a burst of wholesome goodness.

Note: To make these, you will need a flower-shaped silicone baking pan.

MAKES 6 ROLLS

Ingredients

1 package refrigerated cinnamon
  bun dough (found in most
  grocery stores)

1 banana, peeled and cut into
  ½-in-/12-mm-thick slices

¼ cup/45 g golden raisins/
  sultanas

¼ cup/45 g dried apricots, diced

1. Preheat the oven to 350°F/180°C.

2. On a floured surface, roll the dough out to a 12-in/30-cm square. Sprinkle evenly with the banana, raisins/sultanas, and apricots.

3. Cut the dough into six pieces and lightly press each into a flower-shaped mold.

4. Bake for 12 to 15 minutes, or until golden brown. Remove from the oven and transfer the buns from the pan to wire racks to cool. Serve warm or at room temperature.

RECIPE

FAIRY BREAD

Be sure to make lots of this fairy bread; shaped like flowers
and decorated with sugar sprinkles, it won't last long.

· · · · · · · · · · · · · · · · · · ❀ · · · · · · · · · · · · · · · · · · ·

MAKES 12 SERVINGS

Ingredients

12 slices white bread

Unsalted butter, at room
temperature, or Vanilla Icing
(page 29)

Colored sugar sprinkles and
cookie decorations

Using a flower-shaped cookie cutter, cut a shape from each
bread slice. Spread on the butter or icing and sprinkle with
the decorations.

RECIPE

FAIRY BARS

Fairies need lots of fuel, so treat them to one or more kinds of sweet bars: brownies, blondies, and krispy treats.

· ❀ ·

Ingredients

⅓ cup/30 g unsweetened cocoa powder

½ cup/65 g all-purpose/plain flour

¼ tsp salt

¼ tsp baking powder

½ cup/115 g unsalted butter, at room temperature

1 cup/200 g granulated sugar

2 large eggs, beaten

1 tsp vanilla extract/essence

CHOCOLATE FROSTING

3 Tbsp unsalted butter, at room temperature

3 Tbsp unsweetened cocoa powder

1 tsp vanilla extract/essence

1 cup/200 g confectioners'/icing sugar, sifted

BROWNIE BARS
MAKES 12 BARS

1. Preheat the oven to 350°F/180°C. Butter and flour an 8-in/20-cm square baking pan; knock out the excess flour.

2. In a medium bowl, combine the cocoa, flour, salt, and baking powder. Stir with a whisk to blend. In a small saucepan over low heat, or in a microwave, melt the $^{1}/_{2}$ cup/ 115 g butter. In another bowl, stir in the melted butter, the sugar, eggs, and vanilla. Gradually stir in the dry ingredients until smooth. Scrape the batter into the prepared pan and smooth the top.

3. Bake for 25 to 30 minutes, or until a toothpick inserted in the center comes out clean. Remove from the oven and let cool completely on a wire rack.

4. **FOR THE FROSTING:** In a small bowl, combine all the ingredients and beat until smooth.

5. Frost the brownies. Let stand until the frosting is set, about 15 minutes. Cut into 12 bars.

Ingredients

2 ¼ cups/255 g all-purpose/plain flour

2 ½ tsp baking powder

½ tsp salt

¾ cup/170 g unsalted butter,
    at room temperature

1 ¾ cups/350 g packed brown sugar

3 large eggs

1 tsp vanilla extract/essence

2 cups/375 g semisweet/plain
    chocolate chips

Ingredients

3 Tbsp unsalted butter

1 package marshmallows
    (about 40)

6 cups/158 g Rice Krispies

½ cup/85 g golden raisins/
    sultanas

BLONDIE BARS
MAKES 16 BARS

1. Preheat the oven to 350°F/180°C. Coat a 9-by-13-in/ 23-by-33-cm baking pan with cooking spray or melted butter.

2. In a medium bowl, combine the flour, baking powder, and salt. Stir with a whisk to blend. In a large bowl, cream the butter and brown sugar until light and fluffy. Beat in the eggs and vanilla until smooth. Gradually stir in the dry ingredients until smooth. Stir in the chocolate chips. Scrape into the prepared pan and smooth the top.

3. Bake for 20 to 25 minutes, or until golden brown and a toothpick inserted in the center comes out clean. Remove from the oven and let cool completely in the pan on a wire rack. Cut into 16 bars.

RAISINY RICE KRISPY TREATS
MAKES 16 BARS

1. Coat a 9-by-13-in/23-by-33-cm pan with cooking spray or melted butter.

2. In a large saucepan, melt the butter over low heat. Add the marshmallows and stir until completely melted. Remove from the heat. Stir in the cereal and raisins/ sultanas until well coated.

3. Press the mixture into the prepared pan and let cool. Cut into 16 bars.

RAINBOW PARFAITS

This colorful dessert treat is easy to make, is easy to serve,
and appeals to fairies of all ages. Rainbow-colored gelatin is cut
into squares, then artfully arranged by color in small glasses. They look
like little gems in the sunlight and are a favorite of the fairy set.

· ❁ ·

SERVES 6 FAIRIES

Ingredients

One 3-oz/85-g package *each* lime,
blueberry, lemon, orange,
and strawberry gelatin

4 cups/960 ml boiling water

1 cup/240 ml cold water

2 cups/500 ml heavy/
double cream

1 tsp vanilla extract/essence

2 Tbsp sugar

1. Pour one flavor of gelatin into a small bowl and stir in
1 cup/240 ml of the boiling water until dissolved. Pour
in 1/4 cup/60 ml of the cold water and stir. Pour into an
8-in/20-cm or other small square dish. Repeat with the
remaining flavors. Refrigerate for 3 hours until firm.

2. Combine the cream, vanilla, and sugar in a deep bowl. With
an electric mixer, beat on high speed until soft peaks form.

3. Cut the gelatin in each dish into 1-in/2.5-cm squares and
layer the various colors with the whipped cream in each of
six small parfait glasses.

4. Top each dessert with a dollop of whipped cream.

Fairies ROCK

Fairies rock, we never stop.
We're shiny and twirly,
And, of course, we're girly.
Every day and night,
Our dreams take flight.

EVEN THE SWEETEST FAIRIES have

their wild side, and it's clearly shown here as they rock out in their raspberry-colored skirts and tops. The cotton tees have a glittery message, and the bright skirts are bursting with attitude.

This party is geared to older girls, who may have grown out of sweet fairy costumes and will be oh-so-delighted to be musical stars. The party kicks into gear with each girl making her own bloom-adorned shoes. After everyone is dressed in the special garb, the girls perform karaoke songs individually and then in a group. Be sure to have popular songs on hand to keep their interest.

At intermission, the fairies will snack on pizzas, rocktails, tie-dyed cookies, and winged cupcakes. Then, they'll go to the garden or patio for limbo dancing and a musical memory game. At last, the tired rockers exit stage right to rest up for the next show.

COSTUMES

Headbands
Rock Star Skirts
Blossomy Shoes
Glittery Tops

CRAFTS/GAMES

Boa Wands
Lyric Memory Game
Limbo Dancing

RECIPES

Pocketbook Pizzas
Rocktails
Tie-Dyed Shortbread
Fairy Wing Cupcakes

SET THE STAGE with a jewel-toned curtain made from lengths of ribbon found in sale bins at craft stores. (For complete instructions, see page 131.) After the party, this makes a great panel of color in a doorway or on the wall of a girl's bedroom. Add colorful paper stars for an even more dazzling rock-star setting (see page 132 for instructions). Life-size blow-up guitars and microphones (found at party supply stores) make for fun accessories.

HEADBANDS

Easy-on, easy-off headbands are perfect for the active
modern fairy. Made from elasticized ribbon in a vibrant raspberry
shade, they are simply tied together in a knot.

MAKES 6 HEADBANDS

You will need

Scissors

6 yd/540 cm ⅜-in-/1-cm-wide
raspberry-colored
elasticized ribbon

Using the scissors, cut the ribbon into six 1-yd/90-cm
lengths. Wrap a ribbon around each girl's head twice,
like a headband, and tie and knot the ends. Snip off the
excess ribbon.

ROCK STAR SKIRTS

These sassy skirts have a layer of berry-colored tulle, a satin lining,
and a double ruffle at the hem, and are finished with a satin waistband.

MAKES 6 SKIRTS

You will need

Scissors

3 yd/270 cm 36-in-/90-cm-wide
fuchsia satin lining fabric

6 yd/540 cm 36-in-/90-cm-wide
raspberry-colored tulle
(found in rolls in craft stores)

Straight pins

Sewing machine

Matching thread

5 yd/450 cm ½-in-/
12-mm-wide elastic

Safety pin

1. Using the scissors, cut the satin and 3 yd/270 cm of the tulle into six 18-in-/45-cm-long pieces (to yield 12 pieces of cut fabric altogether). Place a piece of satin on a work surface and layer with a piece of tulle on top, leaving 2 in/5 cm of the satin lining showing at the top to fold over for the waistband. Fold the satin over 1 in/2.5 cm at the top to cover the top edge of the tulle, and pin the top satin to the middle tulle, and the bottom satin together. Using the sewing machine, stitch along the pins.

2. Cut the elastic into six 30-in/75-cm lengths. With the safety pin fastened to one end of the elastic, slide a piece of elastic through the top hem. Fold the fabric lengthwise and pin the sides and elastic together to make a 1-in/2.5-cm seam. Stitch along the pins. Remove the pins and turn the skirt right-side out.

3. Cut the remaining 3 yd/270 cm of tulle into eighteen strips, each 6 in/15 cm wide and 1 yd/90 cm long. Layer three strips of tulle together and pin along one long edge, leaving a 1-in/2.5-cm hem. Stitch the strips together. Remove the pins and pull the thread gently to gather the tulle, making an even ruffle. Pin the ruffle to the bottom edge of the tulle of the skirt. Stitch in place. Repeat with the remaining tulle and skirts.

BLOSSOMY SHOES

Fairies who rock are constantly on their feet, so comfortable
shoes are a must. These plastic garden shoes, found in craft stores,
are embellished with raspberry-colored peony blossoms.

MAKES 6 PAIRS OF SHOES

You will need

12 raspberry-colored fabric
    peony blossoms

6 pairs pink plastic garden shoes
    to fit the fairies

    Aleene's Tacky Glue

1. Remove the stems off the peonies so that the bottoms
   are flat.

2. Center a blossom on one shoe of a pair and glue in place.

3. Repeat with the other shoe. Let dry.

4. Repeat with the remaining pairs of shoes and blossoms.
   Let dry.

COSTUME

GLITTERY TOPS

Tops that rock say it all,
in glittery press-on letters.

· ❖ ·

MAKES 6 TOPS

You will need

6 raspberry-colored
    spaghetti-strap tops

Iron and ironing board

Iron-on glitter letters
    (found in craft stores)

1. Place a top on the ironing board.

2. Arrange the glitter letters to read *fairies rock* in the middle of the top. Following the manufacturer's instructions, iron the letters onto the top.

3. Repeat with the remaining tops and letters.

CRAFT

BOA WANDS

Fashioned from neon-colored mini boas wrapped
around Styrofoam balls, these wands are finished off with
shimmery rose petals and ribbons for a star-like quality.

MAKES 6 WANDS

You will need

Sharp scissors

Three 30-in/76-cm ³/₈-in-/1-cm-thick
wooden dowels

Paper towels/absorbent paper

Raspberry-colored acrylic paint

Six 2-in-/5-cm-diameter
Styrofoam balls

6 yd/540 cm bright pink faux
feather boas (found in
craft stores)

Straight pins

Aleene's Tacky Glue

60 fabric rose petals

6 yd/540 cm ¼-in-/6-mm-wide
raspberry-colored ribbon

1. Using the scissors, cut each dowel into two 15-in/38-cm
lengths. Using a paper towel/absorbent paper, rub acrylic
paint onto the dowels to stain.

2. Anchor a Styrofoam ball onto a dowel by pushing firmly
down so that the dowel goes into the ball about 2 in/5 cm.
Repeat with the remaining dowels and balls.

3. Cut the boas into twelve 18-in/45-cm lengths. Pin a length
of boa to the underside of the ball and wrap and glue the boa
on so that the ball is covered with the boa. Pin the end of the
boa to the ball to secure. Pin rose petals to the bottom of the
ball around the dowel. Repeat to make 5 more wands.

4. Cut the ribbon into 12-in/30-cm lengths and tie 3 strands
to each dowel underneath the boa ball.

LYRIC MEMORY GAME

1. Rockers love to play games, especially memory games! For this one, song lyrics are recited to one girl, and then passed on to each successive girl, until the final girl has to guess the name of the song with the lyrics that have been around the ring.

2. The winner gets a disc of party favorites (see page 142), burned on a home computer.

LIMBO DANCING

1. You'll need a long pole or broom handle and two people to hold it, one at each end. And some fun fairy party tunes (see page 142).

2. The fairies line up and take turns limbo dancing under the pole. The pole is lowered after everyone has a pass.

3. Those who touch the pole while passing under it are out of the competition. The winner is the fairy who limbos under the pole at the lowest level.

RECIPE

POCKETBOOK PIZZAS

These pastry "purses" are filled with tomato sauce and cheese.
The handle shape is great for grabbing on the run. For a nutritious
side to the pizzas, put out a plate of sliced cucumber, grape tomatoes,
and mini carrots, with a small dish of ranch dressing for dipping.

MAKES 12 PIZZAS; SERVES 6 FAIRIES

Ingredients

1 package frozen pizza dough,
   thawed

1 cup/250 ml jarred pizza
   or marinara sauce

1½ cups/185 g shredded
   mozzarella cheese

1 large egg white

1. Preheat the oven to 400°F/200°C. Coat a baking sheet/tray with cooking spray.

2. Roll out the pizza dough on a lightly floured surface to a rectangular shape, about 1/4 in/6 mm thick. Cut into twelve squares. On the bottom right-hand corner of a square, put 2 tablespoons of sauce and 2 heaping tablespoons of cheese, leaving a 1/2-in/12-mm border at the edge.

3. Take the right-hand corner and roll it diagonally toward the opposite corner. Take the other two opposite sides, stretch them a bit, and wrap them above the rolled dough to form a handle. Twist the ends together. Repeat with the remaining squares, sauce, and cheese. Place on the prepared pan.

4. In a small bowl, beat the egg white with a whisk until foamy. Using a pastry brush, coat the pocketbooks. Bake for 15 minutes, or until golden brown. Transfer to wire racks to cool slightly. Serve warm.

RECIPE

ROCKTAILS

These refreshing drinks are both delicious and nutritious.
Made from a blend of sparkling water and a splash of
pomegranate juice, they're topped off with Swirly Straws.

SERVES 6 FAIRIES

Ingredients

Ice cubes

2 liters seltzer water

One 10-oz/300-ml bottle
pomegranate juice

6 swirly straws

Fill 6 glasses with ice and add seltzer until two-thirds full.
Top with a splash of pomegranate juice and serve with
the straws.

SWIRLY STRAWS

Cut six 5-in-/12-cm-diameter hot-pink foam rounds into swirl
shapes. Punch a hole in one end of each swirl and insert one
end of a bendable white straw. Cut 1 yd/90 cm of bright pink
faux feather boa into six 6-in/15-cm lengths. Wrap one
length around each swirl and straw.

TIE-DYED SHORTBREAD

A light, fluffy frosting topped with pink and purple tie-dye
swirls makes these shortbreads a most artistic treat.

MAKES 24 COOKIES

Ingredients

1 cup/225 g unsalted butter,
   at room temperature

1 cup/200 g granulated sugar

1 tsp vanilla extract

2 ½ cups/285 g all-purpose/plain flour

¼ tsp salt

Vanilla Icing (page 29)

1 tube purple icing

1 tube pink icing

1. Preheat the oven to 350°F/180°C. Coat a baking sheet/tray with cooking spray.

2. In a medium bowl, cream the butter and sugar together until light and fluffy. Stir in the vanilla. In a medium bowl, combine the flour and salt. Stir with a whisk to blend.

3. Gradually stir the dry ingredients into the butter mixture. On a lightly floured surface, shape the dough into a disk. Place in a self-sealing plastic bag and refrigerate for at least 30 minutes or up to 24 hours.

4. On a floured surface, roll the dough to a thickness of 1/4 in/ 6 mm. Cut out shapes with a 3-in/7.5-cm round cutter. Transfer to the prepared sheet/tray and bake for 15 minutes, or until the edges are golden brown. Remove from the oven and let cool for 10 minutes. Transfer to wire racks to cool completely.

5. Ice the shortbread with the vanilla icing. Put dots of pink and purple icing all over the shortbreads. Using a toothpick, make swirls by connecting the two colors in a tie-dye fashion. Let set for 10 minutes. Store in an airtight container for up to 3 days.

TIME-SAVER: If you're running short on time, use packaged dough, found in the refrigerated section of your grocery store.

RECIPE

FAIRY WING CUPCAKES

These winged wonders, topped with fresh cream,
jam, and colorful sprinkles, are a sure crowd pleaser.

· · · · · · · · · · · · · · · · · ☀ · · · · · · · · · · · · · · · · ·

MAKES 18 CUPCAKES

Ingredients:

1 cup/225 g unsalted butter,
   at room temperature

1 cup/200 g granulated sugar

3 large eggs

1 ½ tsp vanilla extract/essence

2¼ cups/455 g all-purpose/plain flour

¾ tsp baking soda/bicarbonate of soda

½ tsp baking powder

½ tsp salt

½ cup/120 ml buttermilk

3 cups/720 ml heavy/double cream

¼ cup/50 g confectioners'/icing
   sugar, sifted

³⁄₈ cup/85 g raspberry jam

   Pink sugar crystals for sprinkling

1. Preheat the oven to 350°F/180°C. Line 18 standard muffin cups with paper liners.

2. In a large bowl, cream the butter and sugar together until light and fluffy. Beat in the eggs one at a time, then the vanilla.

3. In a medium bowl, whisk the flour, baking soda/bicarbonate of soda, baking powder, and salt. Stir into the butter mixture alternately with the buttermilk in two increments until smooth scraping down the sides of the bowl as needed.

4. Pour the batter into the prepared muffin cups, filling them three-fourths full. Bake for 20 minutes, or until golden brown and a toothpick inserted in the center of a cupcake comes out clean. Remove from the oven and let cool in the pan for 10 minutes. Remove from the pan and let cool completely.

5. Cut a small cone shape, about 1 in/2.5 cm wide at the top, out of the top of each cupcake. Remove the cones and cut each in half lengthwise, forming wings.

6. In a bowl, combine the cream and confectioners'/icing sugar. Beat until soft peaks form. Spoon 1 tsp jam and then 1 tbsp whipped cream into the hole in each cupcake. Add the wings by pressing the pointed edges down into the cream. Sprinkle with pink sugar. Serve now, or refrigerate for up to 24 hours.

Woodland FAIRIES

Mystical things, fairies with wings,
Dance 'round the tree so merrily.
Each barefoot sprite will dance all night,
But with the dawn they cease to be,
Leaving magic dust beneath the tree.

THIS FAIRY PARTY is perfect for girls of all ages. Who doesn't love to feast in the forest and frolic on the moss?

After the girls have changed into their sparkling outfits in the softest hues of green, they'll decorate small bags with ivy tendrils and woodland blossoms to be used for a treasure hunt later. Then the fairies will flit over to their wooded fairyland, where butterflies hover above a table filled with delicacies. Finally, it's off to play fairy games in the enchanted forest.

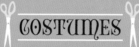

COSTUMES

Flower Crowns

Leafy Skirts

Woodland Tops

Wings

Ribbon Ankle Wraps

CRAFTS/GAMES

Ivy Wands

Treasure Sacks

Treasure Hunt

Sack Races

RECIPES

Strawberry Punch

Sweet Trail Mix

Cupcake Mushrooms

Woodland Pizzas

SET YOUR FAIRYLAND against nature's green backdrop. Twirling spheres of grape-vine filled with clouds of tulle and hung from branches attract butterflies of all shades. Cover the table in a soft layer of tulle topped with tufts of moss to mimic the forest floor. Wrap the chairs and cake stand in tulle for a gauzy look. Arrange trail-mix boxes down the center, then clip on butterflies and add ivy tendrils for the final touch of forest magic.

FLOWER CROWNS

Evoking a simple daisy chain, this crown
is made especially for nature fairies.

· · · · · · · · · · · · · · · ❧ · · · · · · · · · · · · · · ·

MAKES 6 CROWNS

You will need

Wire cutters

3 yd/270 cm paper-covered
   florist's wire

Scissors

6 yd/540 cm ½-in-/12-mm-wide
   cream-colored satin ribbon

Hot-glue gun

Glue sticks

2 packages (about 80 flowers)
   white wire-stemmed flowers
   (found in craft stores)

3 yd/270 cm ⅜-in-/1-cm-wide
   light green grosgrain ribbon

3 yd/270 cm ¼-in-/6-mm-wide
   white satin ribbon

1. Using the wire cutters, cut the floral wire into six 18-in/
   45-cm lengths. Twist each length of wire to form a circle.

2. Using the scissors, cut the cream-colored ribbon into
   1-yd/90-cm lengths. Glue one end of a length of ribbon
   onto the wire circle. Wrap the ribbon around the circle,
   covering the paper. Cut and glue the end of the ribbon to
   the circle. Repeat with the remaining circles.

3. Separate the flowers into individual blooms and wire them
   onto each ribbon-covered crown.

4. Cut the green and white ribbons into 18-in/45-cm lengths.
   Take one green and one white ribbon and tie onto the back
   of each crown, making a knot so that the ribbons dangle
   like streamers.

LEAFY SKIRTS

These billowy pale green skirts will
glitter in the enchanted woods.

· · · · · · · · · · · · · · · · 🦋 · · · · · · · · · · · · · · · ·

MAKES 6 SKIRTS

You will need

Scissors

3 yd/270 cm 36-in-/
90-cm-wide pale green
pearlized sheer fabric

3 yd/270 cm 36-in-/
90-cm-wide pale green tulle
(found in rolls in craft stores)

3 yd/270 cm 36-in-/
90-cm-wide pale green
satin lining fabric

Straight pins

Sewing machine

Matching thread

5 yd/450 cm ¾-in-/
2-cm-wide elastic

Safety pin

1. Using the scissors, cut all three fabrics to 18-in/45-cm lengths. On a work surface, layer one piece of pearlized sheer fabric on the bottom, then top with a piece of tulle, then a piece of lining fabric. Fold over the top 1 in/2.5 cm of all three fabrics and pin. Using the sewing machine, stitch along the pins to make a top hem.

2. Cut the elastic into six 30-in/75-cm lengths. With the safety pin fastened to one end of the elastic, slide it through the hem. Fold the fabric over lengthwise and pin the sides and elastic together to make a 1-in/2.5-cm seam. Stitch along the pins. Remove the pins and turn the skirt right-side out.

3. Repeat to make the remaining 5 skirts.

WOODLAND TOPS

White cotton tops are adorned with just the right
touch of woodland accents for forest sprites.

· · · · · · · · · · · · · · · · · · · ❧ ·

MAKES 6 TOPS

You will need

6 white cotton tops

18 fabric dogwood blossoms

Scissors

1 yd/90 cm ½-in-/12-mm-wide
light green grosgrain ribbon

1 yd/90 cm ¼-in-/6-mm-wide
cream-colored ribbon

Fabric glue

1. Place a top on a work surface.

2. Arrange 3 blossoms in a triangle shape and glue to the top
in the upper left corner.

3. Cut both colors of ribbon into six 6-in/15-cm lengths. Fold
one of each ribbon in half. Tuck the fold under the dogwood
blossoms and glue to the top.

4. Repeat to make the remaining tops.

WINGS

Fairies take flight when
they wear petal-topped wings.

MAKES 6 PAIRS OF WINGS

You will need

6 stems yellow and white
fabric blossoms

Hot-glue gun

Glue sticks

6 pairs white netted store-
bought wings

Scissors

3 yd/270 cm 6-in-/15-cm-
wide white tulle (found
in rolls at craft stores)

1. Remove the blossoms from the stems. Hot-glue the blossoms to a pair of wings in a pleasing pattern.

2. Using the scissors, cut the tulle into six 18-in/45-cm lengths. Wrap a length of tulle around the center where the wings meet and tie into a bow.

3. Repeat with the remaining blossoms, tulle, and pairs of wings.

RIBBON ANKLE WRAPS

No shoes needed here; a ribbon wrap is
just the thing for barefoot sprites.

MAKES 6 WRAPS

You will need

Scissors

3 yd/270 cm ½-in-/12-mm-wide
  light green grosgrain ribbon

2 yd/180 cm 6-in-/15-cm-wide
  white tulle (found in rolls in
  craft stores)

Hot-glue gun

Glue sticks

24 fabric dogwood blossoms

1. Using the scissors, cut the ribbon into six 18-in/45-cm lengths and the tulle into six 12-in/30-cm lengths.

2. Hot-glue 4 dogwood blossoms onto one end of each length of ribbon. Let dry.

3. Wrap the tulle around each fairy ankle, encircle with the ribbon two or three times, and tie in place.

IVY WANDS

Blooming with woodland flowers, ivy tendrils, and tulle,
these are spell-casters for wandering fairies.

MAKES 6 WANDS

You will need

Sharp scissors

Three 30-in/76-cm ³/₈-in-/1-cm-thick
wooden dowels

White spray paint

1 bunch fabric ivy leaves

3 stems fabric dogwood blossoms

Silver florist's wire

6 yd/540 cm 6-in-/15-cm-
wide white tulle (found in rolls
at craft stores)

2 yd/180 cm ½-in-/12-mm-wide
white ribbon

1. Using the scissors, cut each dowel into two 15-in/
38-cm lengths.

2. Spray paint the dowels white and let dry.

3. Cut small sprigs of ivy and stems of dogwood, about 4 in/
10 cm in length, and make small bouquets for each wand.
Use the florist's wire to wire the bouquets onto one end of
each dowel.

4. Cut the tulle into six 1-yd/90-cm lengths. Begin making
small loops around the bouquet on the wand with the tulle,
keeping a firm grip on the bottom as you go around the
stem. When finished, secure the tulle loops to the wand
with florist's wire.

5. Cut the ribbon into six 12-in/30-cm lengths. Wrap a length
of ribbon around the wire to cover it.

6. Repeat to make 5 more wands.

TREASURE SACKS

These tiny treasure carry-alls are perfect
for holding the map or for collecting all the treats
along the way to the treasure.

MAKES 6 SACKS

You will need

6 small canvas bags (found
   in craft stores)

18 fabric dogwood blossoms

18 fabric ivy leaves

   Fabric glue

   Scissors

5 yd/450 cm natural-colored
   raffia

1. Place a bag on a work surface. On the front of the bag, arrange 3 blossoms and 3 leaves in a pleasing pattern.

2. Glue onto the bag. Let dry.

3. Using the scissors, cut three 10-in/25-cm lengths of raffia and tie around one handle of the bag.

4. Repeat to make 5 more sacks.

TREASURE HUNT

1. Make treasure maps by coloring the clues on a sheet of paper and then make color copies. Roll each up and tie with a decorative ribbon.

2. The fairies follow the maps around the yard to sites where clues have been placed, and the first fairy to reach the end of the path wins a small prize (you can also have a small box at the end for a treasure chest, filled with enough treats for all of the party-goers).

SACK RACES

1. To play this game, you'll need a sack for each player, a start and finish line, and a small course for them to navigate. (Old pillowcases were used here for the sacks, but burlap or fabric sacks would work fine as well.)

2. The fairies step into the sacks and, holding them up around their waists, hop from start to finish.

3. The first one to cross the finish line is the winner.

STRAWBERRY PUNCH

Thirst-quenching and colorful, this punch is a winner
with the fairy set. The base can be made ahead of time, and the
sparkling water and ice cubes added just before serving.

SERVES 6 FAIRIES

Ingredients

3 cups/375 g fresh strawberries,
   hulled and quartered,
   plus 4 sliced strawberries
   for garnish

¾ cup/180 ml fresh lemon juice

1 cup/200 g sugar

2 liters sparkling water, chilled

4 cups ice cubes

1. Puree the quartered strawberries in a blender or
food processor. Strain the puree through a fine-mesh
sieve, pushing on the solids with the back of a large
spoon. Pour into a pitcher or punch bowl.

2. Add the lemon juice and sugar and stir well. Pour
in the sparkling water, add the ice cubes, garnish
with the sliced strawberries, and serve.

SWEET TRAIL MIX

Colorful, tasty, and full of crunch, this trail mix is
sure to power-up the sprites and keep them playing for hours.

Note: You will need six take-out boxes for this treat.

MAKES 10 CUPS/780 G; SERVES 6 FAIRIES

Ingredients

- 4 cups/80 g popped popcorn
- 3 cups/180 g pretzel sticks
- 1 cup/185 g M&M's
- 1 cup/185 g chocolate chips
- 1 cup/185 g peanut butter–
  flavored chips

Combine all the ingredients in a large bowl and stir to mix.
Divide evenly among six take-out boxes.

RECIPE

CUPCAKE MUSHROOMS

These oversized chocolate "mushrooms" are
sure to be a fairy favorite. Tint the icing any color
to coordinate with your woodland theme.

. . . .

MAKES 18 CUPCAKES

Ingredients

⅔ cup/60 g unsweetened
  cocoa powder

1 cup/240 ml hot water

2 cups/225 g cake/soft-wheat flour

2 tsp baking soda/bicarbonate
  of soda

½ tsp salt

1 cup/225 g unsalted butter,
  at room temperature

2 cups/400 g packed brown sugar

3 large eggs

2 tsp vanilla extract/essence

4 oz/125 g unsweetened
  chocolate, melted

⅓ cup/80 ml buttermilk

  Vanilla Icing (page 29)
  mixed with a few drops of
  food coloring

  Jumbo confetti sprinkles

1. Preheat the oven to 350°F/180°C. Line 18 standard muffin
   cups with paper liners.

2. In a small bowl, combine the cocoa powder and hot water;
   whisk until smooth. Let cool to room temperature.

3. In a medium bowl, whisk the flour, baking soda/bicarbonate
   of soda, and salt. In a large bowl, cream the butter and brown
   sugar together until light and fluffy. Beat in the eggs, one at
   a time. Add the vanilla. Stir in the melted chocolate.

4. Add the dry ingredients to the butter mixture alternately
   with the buttermilk in two increments, stirring just until
   blended. Add the cocoa mixture and stir just until blended.
   Ladle into the prepared muffin cups, filling them three-
   fourths full.

5. Bake for 18 to 24 minutes, or until risen and set, and a
   toothpick inserted in the center of a cupcake comes out
   clean. Remove from the oven and let cool for 10 minutes.
   Transfer the cupcakes from the pans to wire racks to cool
   completely. Frost the cupcakes, decorate with the confetti
   sprinkles, and let stand for 10 minutes for the icing to set.

WOODLAND PIZZAS

A perfect party meal, quick, easy, and delicious—
what more could you ask for? The pizzas are small enough
that they can be eaten by hand for fairies on the go.

MAKES 12

Ingredients

1 package frozen pizza
    dough, thawed

1 cup/250 ml pizza sauce

1 small zucchini/courgette, sliced

5 small mushrooms, sliced

2 cups/250 g shredded
    mozzarella cheese

1. Preheat the oven to 400°F/200°C. Cut the pizza dough into 12 pieces. On a floured surface, roll each piece into a 4-in-/10-cm-diameter round. Place the rounds on baking sheet/trays. Spread pizza sauce on each round, top with zucchini/courgette and mushroom slices, and sprinkle with the cheese.

2. Bake for 15 minutes, or until the cheese is melted and the crust is a light golden brown. Remove from the oven, let cool slightly on wire racks, and serve warm.

FAIRY CRAFTS

& SETTING THE SCENE

The beauty of a fairy party is that you can mix and match all
sorts of fun activities for your very own event. This section
includes a range of crafts and decor that you can add to the
themed parties in the previous pages. Or, you can simply pick
and choose from what you find here to create a party for your
particular batch of fairies.

CUTIE-PIE CLIPS

Sweet and simple clips and barrettes
add a magical touch to any fairy outfit.

MAKES 6 CLIPS

You will need

Scissors

12 in/30 cm ³⁄₈-in-/1-cm-wide
    grosgrain ribbon in your
    choice of color

6 metal barrettes, about
    2 in/5 cm long and ¼ in/
    6 mm wide

Fabric glue

18 small fabric appliqué flowers,
    about ¾ in/2 cm wide
    with flat bottoms

1. Using the scissors, cut a piece of ribbon the exact length of the barrette and glue it to the top. Let the glue dry completely, about 3 minutes.

2. Glue the flowers onto the barrette, either spaced evenly or bunched as you like. Let the glue dry completely.

SERENDIPITY BRACELETS

Create magical messages with silver letter beads.

MAKES 6 BRACELETS

You will need:

Scissors

1 package (3 yd/270 cm)
   rainbow-hued elastic cording

3 packages silver block
   letter beads

1. Using the scissors, cut the elastic cording into 6-in/ 15-cm lengths.

2. Arrange the letters into words that will form phrases like *fairies rule* and *good fairies*. String the letters onto the cording. String one word, make a knot, and tie off the first bracelet. Then string the second word to form the complete phrase.

3. Tie the ends of the cordings into tight knots and trim the ends.

JEWELED FLIP-FLOPS

This is a fancy treat for little feet, with gems complete.

MAKES 6 PAIRS

You will need

6 pairs white rubber flip-flops

Scissors

2 ½ yd/225 cm ⅜-in-/1-cm-wide bright pink grosgrain ribbon

Hot-glue gun

Glue sticks

2 ½ yd/225 cm light-pink sequin trim

6 yd/540 cm 6-in-/15-cm-wide pink tulle (found in rolls in craft stores)

3 packages hot-pink sequin trim

1. Measure the rubber strip on the flip-flops and, using the scissors, cut the grosgrain ribbon into pieces the same length. Hot-glue the ribbon pieces along the rubber strip. Repeat with the remaining flip-flops. Let dry.

2. Measure, cut, and glue the light-pink sequin trim on top of the ribbon. Repeat with the remaining flip-flops. Let dry.

3. Cut the tulle into 18-in/45-cm lengths. Lay a length of tulle on a work surface and fold it over, accordion-style, into five 3-in/7.5-cm lengths. Cut off the remaining piece of tulle and use it to tie the folded tulle together in the center. Cut the loop ends to create a puff. Repeat to make eleven more puffs.

4. Cut the hot-pink sequin trim into twelve 6-in/15-cm lengths. Tie a length around each puff in the center. Glue the puffs onto the flip-flops where the strips meet. Let dry.

PRETTY POCKETBOOKS

These fanciful pocketbooks are perfect for fashionable fairies.

MAKES 6 POCKETBOOKS

You will need

Scissors

6 yd/540 cm 6-in-/15-cm-
wide pink tulle (found in
rolls in craft stores)

2 yd/180 cm ¾-in-/2-cm-wide
purple satin ribbon

Sewing needle

Light pink thread

6 felt pocketbooks (found
at craft stores)

6 stems pink fabric
hydrangea blossoms

Hot-glue gun

Glue sticks

1. Using the scissors, cut the tulle into six 1-yd/90-cm lengths.

2. Take one length of tulle and fold it over, accordion-style, into five 6-in/15-cm lengths. Cut off the remaining piece of tulle and use it to tie the folded tulle together in the center. Cut the loop ends to create a puff.

3. Cut the purple ribbon into six 12-in/30-cm lengths. Make a bow with one length. Take the ends of the tulle used to tie the puff and tie the bow onto the puff. Repeat to make the remaining puffs.

4. With the needle and thread, stitch a puff onto a pocketbook in the upper left corner. Repeat with the remaining puffs and pocketbooks.

5. Remove small bunches of hydrangea blossoms from the stems. Hot-glue them onto the tulle puff and bag for a blossoming effect.

FAIRY FUN TEES

Keep your sprite in fashion with this fairy fun tee.
Add sparkly wings and a tulle fabric skirt for an ethereal effect.

. . . . ✳ . . . .

MAKES 6 TEES

You will need

6 long-sleeved cotton tees

one 12-in/30-cm square cardboard

Fabric marker

Fabric paint in vibrant pink
and purple

Scissors

½ yd/45 cm purple tulle

½ yd/45 cm light pink tulle

Sewing needle

Light pink thread

1. Lay a tee on a work surface. Place the cardboard inside the tee under the front of the tee.

2. Using the fabric marker, lightly outline a dancing fairy. (You can easily find images of fairies online; www. webweaver.nu/clipart/fairies.shtml has a good selection.) Cover the outline of the fairy's body with pink fabric paint, then outline the wings with purple paint. Let dry.

3. Repeat with the remaining tees.

4. Using the scissors, cut the purple tulle into 2-in/5-cm squares and the pink tulle into 2-by-3-in/5-by-7.5-cm rectangles. Layer two pieces of tulle, one purple on top of one pink. Bunch the top edges together to form a light gather, and sew together with the needle and thread. Repeat with the remaining tulle.

5. Sew the ruffles to the tees, making the fairy skirts.

CRAFT

FAIRY FRAMES

Capture precious memories with this hand-painted frame.

MAKES 6 FRAMES

You will need

Six 5-by-7-in/12-by-17-cm
     unfinished wood frames

one jar white acrylic paint

  2 foam brushes

     Paper towels/absorbent paper

  1 jar light pink acrylic paint

     Pencil

  1 small acrylic paint brush
     with pointed tip

  1 bottle Mod Podge sealer

     Hot-glue gun

     Glue sticks

  6 packages pastel gems
     (found in craft stores)

     Scissors

  4 yd/360 cm ³⁄₈-in-/
     1-cm-wide pink gingham–
     checked ribbon

  3 yd/270 cm 6-in/15-cm-wide
     light pink tulle (found in rolls
     in craft stores)

1. On a work surface, paint the frames white using the acrylic paint and foam brushes. Let dry. Paint with a second coat if necessary. Using a paper towel/absorbent paper, gently rub on the light pink paint to stain the frames. Let dry.

2. Pencil in the words *fairies are forever friends* and then paint over the pencil marks with pink paint using the pointed-tip brush. Let dry. Coat the frame with the sealer and let dry.

3. Hot-glue on the gems to dot the *i*'s and then glue more gems on the frame in your desired patterns.

4. Using the scissors, cut the gingham-checked ribbon into twelve 12-in/30-cm pieces. Cut the tulle into twelve 9-in/23-cm pieces.

5. Lay a piece of checked ribbon on top of the tulle. Fold the two pieces over accordion style into 4-in/10-cm lengths.

6. Cut off a 2-in-/5-cm-long piece of the gingham-checked ribbon and tie the folded material together tightly in the center. Fluff out the blossom. Repeat to make twelve puffs.

7. Glue two puffs onto each frame.

MAGICAL FAIRY DUST

Sparkling magic dust glistens inside this decorative
glass jar, just waiting to make wishes come true. (Make sure
that the fairies use this magic dust outside only.)

MAKES 6 JARS

You will need

One 4-oz/125-g package
lavender glitter

Six 2-oz/55-g packages pink and
purple paper confetti

Six 4-oz/115-g cork-topped
decorative glass jars
(found in craft stores)

Fine-point purple
permanent marker

6 cream-colored adhesive labels

Scissors

2 yd/180-cm ¼-in-/6-mm-wide
purple satin ribbon

1. In a small bowl, mix the glitter and confetti together.
   Divide evenly among the jars and secure each tightly
   with the cork.

2. Using the marker, write *Magical Fairy Dust* on each label.
   Affix the labels to the jars.

3. Cut the ribbon into twelve 6-in/15-cm lengths. Tie two
   ribbons around the neck of each bottle. Make a bow,
   if desired.

FAIRY BOWER

Create an enchanting hideaway with billowing layers of tulle
draped over a frame and hung from a tree or an overhead lattice.

MAKES 1 BOWER

You will need

Hot-glue gun

Glue sticks

6 yd/540 cm 2-in-/5-cm-wide
cream-colored satin ribbon

One 30-inch-/76-cm-diameter
hula hoop (found in
toy stores)

Scissors

5 yd/450 cm 1-in-/2.5-cm-wide
cream-colored satin ribbon

8 yd/720 cm 36-in-/90-cm-
wide pink tulle (found in rolls
in craft stores)

2 yd/180 cm 6-in-/15-cm-
wide deep pink tulle (found in
rolls in craft stores)

Safety pins

1. Glue one end of the 2-in-/5-cm-wide ribbon onto the hula hoop. Wrap the ribbon around the hoop to cover it completely, gluing in a few places to secure. Fold over the end and hot-glue it to the hoop.

2. Using the scissors, cut the 1-in-/2.5-cm-wide satin ribbon into three 1-yd/90-cm lengths. In three points equidistant around the hoop, tie one end of each piece of this ribbon to the hoop. Bring the three loose ends of the ribbons together evenly in the center of the hoop and tie in a knot. Check to make sure the hoop hangs evenly from the knot.

3. Lay the hoop on a work surface with the knot in the center. Cut the pink tulle into two 4-yd/360-cm lengths and lay one over the hoop so that the sides are even. Repeat with the other piece of tulle. Take the center point and cut an X through both layers of tulle. Slip the knot through the hole.

4. Cut the deep pink tulle into two 1-yd/90-cm pieces. Fold one piece, accordion style, into six 6-in/15-cm lengths.

(continued)

5. Take a 12-in/30-cm piece of the 1-in/2.5-cm-wide cream-colored ribbon and tie the folded tulle tightly in the center. Fluff out the tulle blossom. Repeat with the remaining tulle piece and cream-colored ribbon.

6. Using safety pins, attach the tulle blossoms to the hoop.

7. Position the 1-in/2.5-cm cream-colored ribbon on the edge of the hoop and pin in place with a safety pin so the ribbon drapes slightly. Continue around the outer edge of the bower pinning every 12 in/30 cm or so.

8. Take the knot and hang the bower from a tree limb by slipping it onto a branch, or by tying the knot onto the metal frame of a patio awning.

RIBBON CURTAIN

Jewel-toned ribbons make a fairy screen for a bedroom or playroom.
Vary the colors to match the color scheme for your party.

· · · · · · · · · · · · · · · · · · · ✳ ·

MAKES 1 CURTAIN

You will need

3 yd/270 cm ½-in/12-mm-wide pink or purple ribbon for the top

Scissors

120 yd/108 m ribbon in assorted shades of pink and purple and assorted widths, if you like

Hot-glue gun

Glue sticks

1. Lay the 3-yd/270-cm length of ribbon on a work surface.

2. Using the scissors, cut the other ribbons into sixty 2-yd/180-cm lengths. Starting 6 in/15 cm in from the end, lay a few ribbon strips perpendicular to the top ribbon and 1 in/2.5 cm apart. Push the ends of the ribbons under the top ribbon and fold them over. Hot-glue in place. Let dry.

3. Continue until all of the strips are glued, leaving 6 in/15 cm free on the other end of the top ribbon.

4. Using the ribbon on each end, hang the curtain wherever you would like a splash of color.

PAPER STARS

Paper stars create a magical canopy of color
for rainbow-hued fairies to frolic under.

MAKES 1 PAPER STAR

You will need:

6 paper bags in *each* color:
pink, blue, green, orange,
yellow, purple

Scissors

Double-sided tape

Hole punch

6 in/15 cm string

1 yd/90 cm white ribbon
or raffia for hanging

1. Fold over the bottom of each bag onto itself. Using the scissors cut above the lower fold, cutting away the bottom of the bag.

2. Cut the sides of each bag to resemble a leaf with a pointed end.

3. Lay the bags in a stack. Turn one bag over and put a strip of double-sided tape on it from the point to the flat bottom. Flip the bag over so that the top two bags are taped together. Place another strip of tape on the second bag and flip over so that the next two are taped together. Continue until all six bags are taped together.

4. At the center of the flat end, use the hole punch to punch a hole through all of the bags. Push the string through and tie the bags together.

5. Place a strip of tape on the top bag, unfold the bags like an accordion, and press the two ends together to form a star.

6. Punch a hole in one of the points of the star and tie the ribbon in a knot. Hang in the party space, from the ceiling, a patio awning, or a tree limb.

BLOOMING GLOBE

Colorful layered blooms abound on this sphere. Make a few
in different sizes and hang in the bedroom, bathroom, or playroom.

MAKES 1 GLOBE

You will need

4 stems fabric flowers

Hot-glue gun

Glue sticks

One 6-in/15-cm Styrofoam ball

4 straight pins or 1 florist's pin

3 yd/270 cm ½-in-/12-mm-wide
coordinating ribbon

1. Remove the fabric blossoms from the stems.

2. Glue the blossoms all over the Styrofoam to cover the
ball completely.

3. Using the straight pins or florist's pin, affix one end of the
ribbon to a point on the ball, pressing firmly down.

4. Use the end of the ribbon to hang the ball.

WIRE HEART

Form soft craft wire into a heart shape and fill it with bits of colorful ribbons and fabrics. Hang on closet doors, desk drawers, or a bedpost for a delightful fairy whimsy.

MAKES 1 HEART

You will need

One 24-in/60-cm length heavy-gauge crafting wire

Pliers

10 ft/300 cm ½-in-/12-mm-wide ribbon or fabric strips

1. Bend the wire into a heart shape. Using the pliers, twist the ends around each other to secure.

2. Tie on 9 ft/270 cm of the ribbon or the fabric strips until the entire wire base is covered.

3. In the top of the heart, make a loop with the remaining 12-in/30-cm length of ribbon. Knot the ends to secure.

4. Hang the wire heart.

FAIRY GAMES

Organizing party games for excited children is no small task, so have your games set up and ready to go. Choose games that appeal to the age group: easier games, such as Pin the Petal on the Flower, for the younger set; and more challenging ones, such as the Memory Game, for the older fairies. Always ask the children which was their favorite game.

Prizes need not be expensive; small tokens, stickers, lip balms, pencils, or notebooks are always popular. If possible, hand out a small prize to each player as she is eliminated; this keeps everyone happy and interested in the game until the end.

Following are a few ideas for games other than the ones featured in the parties themselves.

PIN THE RIBBON TAIL
ON THE FAIRY WINGS

Fairies of all ages will be enchanted with this
version of Pin the Tail on the Donkey. Whoever places her
ribbon tail closest to the center of the wings is the winner.

You will need

One 24-by-36-in/60-by-
90-cm piece of white felt

One 30-in/76-cm ³⁄₈-in-/1-cm-
diameter wooden dowel

Hot-glue gun

Glue sticks

Scissors

Five 9-by-12-in/23-by-30-cm
felt squares: 3 light pink,
1 bright pink, and 1 purple

Fabric glue

6 yd/540 cm ³⁄₈-in-/1-cm-wide
grosgrain ribbon in shades
of purple and pink

2 ft/60 cm 6-in-/15-cm-wide
light pink tulle (found in
rolls in craft stores)

1 package Velcro strips

1. Lay the white felt on a work surface. Lay the dowel across
the top (24-in/60-cm side) and fold the felt toward you to
form a loop around the dowel. Hot-glue the felt in place.
Let dry.

2. Turn the felt to the opposite side. Using the scissors, cut
two of the light pink felt squares into wing shapes and use
the fabric glue to glue to the white felt. Cut ten 3-in/7.5-cm
circles from the bright pink felt square and glue to the wings.

3. Cut 3-in/7.5-cm strips with a scalloped edge from the purple
felt and glue to the bottom edge of the white felt as shown
in the photo.

4. Cut the pink ribbon into two 18-in/45-cm lengths and tie one
piece onto each end of the dowel. Tie the ends of the ribbon
together to form the loop from which to hang the felt.

5. Fold the tulle, accordion-style, into three 6-in/15-cm lengths.
Cut off the remaining piece of tulle and use it to tie the
folded tulle together in the center. Fluff out to make a puff.
Hot-glue onto the center of the wing.

(continued)

6. Cut the third light pink felt square into six 1-by-3-in/ 2.5-by-7.5-cm pieces. Cut the remaining pink and all of the purple ribbon into 12-in/30.5-cm lengths. Gather a group of four ribbons and lay them flat, fold the felt piece over the center of the ribbons, and glue as shown in the photo. Let dry. Adhere a piece of Velcro to the back of the felt; this will allow the ribbon tail to stick to the felt background.

7. Take any remaining pink and purple ribbons and tie them on the ends of the dowel. Hang the game from the ribbon loop so that the wings are eye level with the players.

8. Start the game by blindfolding the first player, turning her around once and pointing her in the direction of the wings.

PIN THE PETAL ON THE FLOWER

This game works like the ribbon tails on the wings;
each girl gets a felt petal, and the girl who pins it
closest to the center of the flower wins.

You will need

One 24-by-36-in/60-by-90-cm piece of white felt

One 30-in/76-cm 3/8-in-/1-cm-diameter wooden dowel

Hot-glue gun

Glue sticks

Scissors

Six 9-by-12-in/23-by-30-cm felt squares, one in each color: yellow, green, brown, pink, purple, and blue

Fabric glue

1 yd/90 cm 3/8-in-/1-cm-wide yellow grosgrain ribbon

1 package Velcro strips

1. Lay the white felt on a work surface. Lay the dowel across the top (24-in/60-cm side) and fold the felt toward you to form a loop around the dowel. Hot-glue the felt in place. Let dry.

2. Turn the felt to the opposite side. Using the scissors, cut out a 3-in/7.5-cm circle from the yellow felt, a 2-by-12-in/ 5-by-30-cm stem from the green felt, and an 8-in-/17-cm-tall flowerpot from the brown felt.

3. Cut out two petal shapes each from the pink, purple, and blue felt.

4. Starting at the bottom center edge of the white felt, use the fabric glue to glue on the brown flowerpot, then the green stem, and then the yellow flower center.

5. Tie one end of the ribbon onto one end of the dowel, tie a knot and repeat on the other side to form a loop to hang so the yellow center is eye level with the players.

6. Place an adhesive Velcro piece on the back of each petal.

7. Start the game by blindfolding the first player, turning her around once, and pointing her in the direction of the flower pot.

GAME

MEMORY GAME

1. Arrange about a dozen different objects on a tray, such as pencils, small toys, rings, and toy cars. Cover the tray with a dish towel and place the tray in front of the children. Uncover the tray for 15 seconds to show them the contents, then cover it up, and ask them to write down all the objects they remember.

2. To play several rounds, you can add objects and ask the players to identify the new ones, or swap out objects and ask them to remember what is missing and what is new.

3. For little ones, use six or so simple objects, like a party hat, a blower, and an invitation; take one away and see if they remember what is missing.

GUESS HOW MANY

1. In this classic game, a jar is filled with colorful candy, gumballs, or beads.

2. Have the kids guess the number of objects in the jar and write it down.

3. The one with the closest number wins the jar.

MAYPOLE AND MAYPOLE DANCE

Set this up on the lawn and let the children
dance to any music you choose.

MAKES 1 MAYPOLE

You will need

White spray paint

Two 6-in/15-cm wooden disks
(found in craft stores)

One 8-ft-/240-cm-long
2-in-/5-cm-wide white
wooden drapery rod

1 wooden finial

Electric drill

2 ½ yd/225 cm 1-in-/2.5-cm-wide
grosgrain ribbon in *each* of
the following colors: light pink,
bright pink, purple, orange,
yellow, blue, and green

Staple gun

One 3-in/7.5-cm double-
sided screw

1 patio umbrella stand

1. Spray paint the disks, drapery rod, and finial white. Let dry. Use the electric drill to drill a $1/2$-in/12-mm hole in the center of each disk, as well as in the top of one end of the drapery rod.

2. Lay the ribbons on a work surface. Position the ends coming out from the center of one disk, spacing them evenly.

3. Use the staple gun to staple the ribbons in place in the center and then on the edges of the disk.

4. Insert the screw in the top of the pole, add the ribbon-covered disk and then the other disk (by slipping them onto the screw) and top with the finial. Twist the finial until it feels tight and the disks are secure.

5. Place the rod in a patio umbrella stand that has been secured to the ground to keep it from toppling over.

6. Start the dance with a curtsy. Every other dancer begins weaving in and out of the dancers standing still. This creates a weave pattern in the ribbons on the pole. As the ribbons tighten, the stationary dancers will be drawn to the center. Then the dancers reverse the weaving until the ribbon is unwound, and the stationary dancers take their turn.

RESOURCES

A. C. MOORE
www.acmoore.com
Faux flowers, paper and paper crafts, framing materials, beading, bridal decorations, seasonal decorations, yarn, and children's crafts.

A. I. FRIEDMAN
www.aifriedman.com
Faux flowers, paper and paper crafts, and a large selection of crafting supplies, including glues, foam sheets, and felt.

DICK BLICK ART SUPPLIES
www.dickblick.com
A wide variety of crafts supplies.

JOANN FABRICS
www.joann.com
Arts and crafts supplies, paper, cards, fabric, scrapbooking materials, and more.

KATE'S PAPERIE
www.katespaperie.com
Stickers, stamps, paper-crafting supplies, ribbon, wrapping papers, and a vast selection of decorative and specialty papers.

KOHL'S
www.kohls.com
Large selection of children's tights and tops.

MICHAELS
www.michaels.com
Kids' crafts, kits, yarn, fiber crafts, floral decorations, seasonal decorations, framing materials, bridal decorations, and scrapbooking.

M & J TRIMMING
www.mjtrim.com
Ribbons, sequined trim, lace, beaded trim, fringes, leather trim, and decorative appliqués.

NEW YORK CAKE AND BAKING SUPPLIES
www.nycake.com
Cookie cutters, shaped and novelty cake pans, bakeware, doilies, and decorative sugars.

ORIENTAL TRADING COMPANY
www.orientaltrading.com
Party supplies and crafts kits for kids.

PEARL RIVER
www.pearlriver.com
Chinese-inspired paper and floral garlands, lanterns, slippers, and decorative accessories.

RAG SHOP
www.ragshop.com
Arts and crafts supplies, paper, and paper crafting supplies.

TARGET
www.target.com
Tops, tights, ballerina slippers, sneakers, and a large selection of crafts and party supplies.

FAIRY MUSIC

"Dance of Sugarplum Fairy"
The Hit Crew

"Drama Queen"
Lindsay Lohan

"A Dream Is a Wish Your Heart Makes"
Ilene Woods

"Ever Ever After"
Carrie Underwood

"Fly to Your Heart"
Selena Gomez

"Fly with Me"
Kari Kimmel

"Happy Working Song"
Amy Adams

"How to Believe"
Ruby Summer

"Let Your Heart Sing"
Katherine McPhee

"Once Upon a Dream"
Emily Osment

"Paint the Sky with Stars"
Enya

"Shine"
Tiffany Giardina

"Some Day My Prince Will Come"
Ashley Tisdale

"So This Is Love"
Cheetah Girls

"That's How You Know"
Amy Adams

"To the Fairies They Draw Near"
Loreena McKennitt

"True Love's Kiss"
Amy Adams & James Marsden

"True to Your Heart"
KeKe Palmer

CD COMPILATIONS

Fairy Nightsongs
Gary Stadler/Sing Kaur

A Flower Fairy Alphabet
Cicely Mary Barker

Tinker Bell
Disney Fairies

INDEX

ACKNOWLEDGMENTS

One little idea can only become a reality with the help and support of so many, and a little fairy dust...

I would like to thank little girls everywhere who find something magical in fairies.

A special thank-you to Jack Deutsch, my fabulous photographer, who worked tirelessly every day to capture the magic in the moment. And to Laura Maffeo, stylist like none other, who saw my vision and helped it come to life.

To my fairies, who were so happy and delighted to put on the costumes and dance in the fairy ring: Alison, Clare, Hayden, Alexandra, Kyra, Julia, Jordan, Hope, Claudia, Grace, and Katie.

To my girlfriends, for all of their support, especially Bets who generously offered her yard to be transformed into fairylands.

To my dear Bertha, whose magic on the sewing machine is unsurpassed.

To my family, who once again lived through the madness of blossoms and tutus everywhere, the hectic crafting process, and the crazy days of shooting. They are my support, and they allow me to soar with magic on my wings.

To my editors at Chronicle, they were tremendous at letting me forge ahead with my creative vision.

To my team at AAM who have taught me in a very short time period that it is impossible to do it all alone, but together magical things can happen.